Contents

SO-CCF-298

Gift-Giving Tips

Unwrapping a homemade present in a beautifully hand-crafted package is one of life's greatest pleasures. *Christmas Gifts from the Kitchen* makes creating these special gifts easier than ever before. Each recipe has detailed preparation steps and a full-color photograph illustrating innovative packaging ideas. Delight your family and friends by giving the most meaningful gift of all—one crafted by hand that's from the heart.

THE PERFECT PACKAGE

Homemade gifts are made extraordinary when tucked into unique packages lavished with decorative accessories. Craft, stationery and kitchen supply stores carry a wide variety of supplies that can add a special touch to your gifts.

Airtight Canisters: These containers are available in a variety of materials, including glass and plastic. They are great for storing snack mixes, cookies and candies.

Baskets: These versatile hold-alls are available in a wide variety of materials and sizes. Large, sturdy ones are well suited for packing entire gift themes. Oblong shapes are wonderful for breads and smaller versions are just right for cookies and candy.

Bottles: Assorted airtight bottles etched with decorative patterns are perfect for barbecue sauces. Always choose securely stoppered bottles to help prevent any leakage.

Boxes: Boxes come in a variety of shapes and sizes and are well suited for cookies, candies, snack mixes and truffles. Large boxes are perfect for packing entire gift themes.

Gift Bags: These handy totes come in a variety of sizes. Pack individual cookies and caramels in smaller bags, and goodie-filled bottles, jars and canisters in larger bags.

Glass Jars: Jars are perfect for packing mustards and snack mixes. Be sure to pack more perishable items, such as sauces, chutneys and jams, in jars with airtight lids.

Packing Peanuts and Bubble Wrap: When shipping your baskets these items are essential. Wrapping all breakable containers in bubble wrap and filling boxes with packing peanuts will help avoid damage during shipping.

Pails: Plastic and metal pails are the right choice for holding smaller items such as snack mixes and candies.

Tins: Metal containers with tight-fitting lids are just the right thing for snack mixes, breads, candies and truffles, and they hold up well when sent through the mail.

FINISHING TOUCHES

After the goodies are made and tucked into decorative packages, you are ready to put the finishing touches on your gift.

Cellophane: An indispensable material for hard-to-wrap gifts such as plates of food, individual breads and candies. Gather the ends and secure with satiny ribbons for a pretty finish.

Decorative Papers: Papers come in a variety of finishes, including glossy and metallic, and many can be enhanced with rubber stamps. Colorful tissue papers are perfect for tucking into gift boxes, bags and pails and are a good substitute for wrapping paper. Or, for a variation on gift wrapping, try gluing paper onto boxes and lids and securing the covered boxes with cords or strings.

Gift Tags: Assorted metal and paper tags come in handy when making personalized notes and cards for your gifts. They also make great labels for storing directions.

Clockwise from top right: Baskets, Canisters, Jars, Packing Peanuts, Gift Bags, Pails, Tins, Boxes and Bottles

Clockwise from top: Tissue Papers, Decorative Papers, Raffia, Rubber Stamps and Ink Pads, Gift Tags, Ribbons and Cellophane

Raffia: Tuck assorted colors of raffia into boxes, baskets and pails. Or, use it as ribbon and tie boxes and tins with pretty bows.

Ribbons, Satin Cords and Strings: Thick colorful ribbons, metallic strings and thin shiny cords are perfect accents for homemade wrapping papers. Make packages more whimsical by tying them with a rainbow of ribbons. Or, spruce up durable cookies by stacking and tying them together with a cord or metallic string.

Rubber Stamps and Ink Pads: Stamps with holiday or food themes paired with colorful inks are perfect for decorating plain papers or wrapping and making personalized note cards for recipes, labels for sauces and jams, storing directions, and gift tags.

SPECIAL INSTRUCTIONS

Before you give your gifts, did you remember to include:

Storage directions? They are included at the end of every recipe and it's a good idea to include them with your gifts. Storage directions are an absolute must for perishable items and those that must be held in the refrigerator.

Serving notes and suggestions? Valuable serving tips are included at the end of some of the recipes, and many photographs illustrate innovative serving suggestions and uses for your edible gifts.

CHOCOLATE TECHNIQUES

MELTING CHOCOLATE

Make sure the utensils used for melting chocolate are completely dry. Moisture will cause the chocolate to "seize," meaning it will become stiff and grainy. If this happens, add ½ teaspoon shortening (not butter) for each ounce of chocolate and stir until smooth. Chocolate will scorch easily, and once scorched cannot be used. Use one of the three following methods for successful melting:

Double Boiler: This is the safest method because it prevents scorching. Place the chocolate in the top of a double boiler or in a heatproof bowl over hot, not boiling water; stir chocolate until smooth. (Make sure that the water remains just below a simmer and is one inch below the bottom of the top pan.) Be careful that no steam or water gets into the chocolate.

Direct Heat: Place the chocolate in a heavy saucepan and melt over very low heat, stirring constantly. Remove the chocolate from heat as soon as it is melted. Be sure to watch the chocolate carefully because it scorches easily when using this method.

Microwave Oven: Place an unwrapped 1-ounce square or 1 cup of chips in a small microwavable bowl. Microwave on HIGH 1 to 1½ minutes, stirring after 1 minute. Stir the chocolate at 30-second intervals until smooth. Be sure to stir microwaved chocolate since it may retain its original shape even when melted.

TEMPERING CHOCOLATE

Melted real chocolate must go through a process of cooling and heating called tempering to avoid blooming. You'll need a candy thermometer for this process. Here's how to temper chocolate:

1. Cover an ordinary heating pad with a towel; place on countertop. Turn the pad to its lowest setting.

2. Grate or finely chop chocolate. Place ¾ of chocolate in the top of a double boiler. Melt over hot, not boiling water. Stir until chocolate has melted.

3. Attach candy thermometer to side of pan, making sure bulb is submerged in chocolate but not touching bottom of pan. Chocolate should be between 110° and 120°F. (Do not let chocolate heat above 120°F.)

4. Remove top of double boiler, being careful not to let steam from bottom of double boiler get near chocolate, and place on towel-covered heating pad. Turn heating pad off. Add remaining ¼ chocolate, 1 tablespoon at a time, stirring gently until it melts. Stir until chocolate has cooled to between 86° and 90°F.

5. The chocolate is now ready for dipping. Check the temperature of the chocolate regularly as you stir and dip. Adjust the temperature of the chocolate by turning the heating pad on and off momentarily. The chocolate's temperature should remain between 86° and 90°F.

Note: If the chocolate rises above 92°F, the temper will be lost and you must begin again.

Savory Snackin' Sensations

Tart Cherry and Almond Sugar Plums

   1 cup (about 6.5 ounces) dried tart
       cherries
   1 cup slivered almonds
   5 teaspoons kirsch (cherry liqueur)
   ⅔ cup coarse white or colored sugar

1. Line medium baking dish with waxed paper; set aside.

2. Place cherries, almonds and kirsch in food processor; process until mixture is finely chopped and comes together.

3. Place sugar in small bowl. Butter hands lightly. Form fruit mixture into 1-inch balls. Roll balls, one at a time, in sugar to coat evenly. Place in prepared pan without touching each other. Let stand 20 to 30 minutes or until firm. Cover tightly and refrigerate up to 3 days.

Makes about 20 balls

Tart Cherry and Almond Sugar
Plums and Apricot-Cranberry-
Walnut Sugar Plums (page 8)

Cranberry-Orange Snack Mix

2 cups oatmeal cereal squares
2 cups corn cereal squares
2 cups mini pretzels
1 cup whole almonds
¼ cup butter
⅓ cup frozen orange juice concentrate, thawed
3 tablespoons packed brown sugar
1 teaspoon ground cinnamon
¾ teaspoon ground ginger
¼ teaspoon ground nutmeg
⅔ cup dried cranberries

1. Preheat oven to 250°F. Spray 13×9-inch baking pan with nonstick cooking spray.

2. Combine cereal squares, pretzels and almonds in large bowl; set aside.

3. Melt butter in medium microwavable bowl on HIGH 45 to 60 seconds. Stir in orange juice concentrate, brown sugar, cinnamon, ginger and nutmeg until blended. Pour over cereal mixture; stir well to coat. Place in prepared pan and spread to one layer.

4. Bake approximately 50 minutes, stirring every 10 minutes. Stir in cranberries.

Let cool in pan on wire rack, leaving uncovered until mixture is crisp. Store in airtight container or resealable plastic food storage bag. *Makes 8 cups*

Apricot-Cranberry-Walnut Sugar Plums

½ cup (about 3 ounces) dried apricots
½ cup (about 3 ounces) dried cranberries
½ cup walnut pieces
¼ teaspoon ground nutmeg
2 tablespoons plus 2 teaspoons orange liqueur
⅔ cup coarse white or colored sugar

1. Line medium baking dish with waxed paper; set aside.

2. Place apricots, cranberries, walnuts, nutmeg and orange liqueur in food processor; process until mixture is finely chopped and comes together.

3. Place sugar in small bowl. Butter hands lightly. Form fruit mixture into 1-inch balls. Roll in sugar to coat evenly. Place in prepared pan. Let stand 20 to 30 minutes or until firm. Cover tightly and refrigerate up to 3 days. *Makes about 20 balls*

Cranberry-Orange Snack Mix

Soft Pretzels

1¼ cups milk
4 to 4½ cups all-purpose flour, divided
¼ cup sugar
1 package active dry yeast
1 teaspoon baking powder
1 teaspoon garlic salt
½ cup unsalted butter, melted
2 quarts water
2 tablespoons baking soda
Coarse salt, sesame seeds, or poppy seeds

1. Heat milk in small saucepan over low heat until temperature reaches 120°F to 130°F.

2. Combine 3 cups flour, sugar, yeast, baking powder and garlic salt in large bowl. Add milk and butter. Beat vigorously 2 minutes. Add remaining flour, ¼ cup at a time, until dough begins to pull away from sides of bowl.

3. Turn out dough onto lightly floured surface; flatten slightly. Knead 10 minutes or until smooth and elastic, adding flour if necessary to prevent sticking.

4. Shape dough into ball. Place in large lightly oiled bowl; turn dough over once to oil surface. Cover with towel; let rise in warm place about 30 minutes.

5. Divide dough into 18 equal pieces. Roll each piece into 22-inch long rope on lightly oiled surface. Form the rope into a "U" shape. About 2 inches from each end, cross the dough. Cross a second time. Fold the loose ends up to the rounded part of the "U"; press the ends to seal. Turn the pretzels over so that the ends are on the underside and reshape if necessary. Cover with towel; let rest 20 minutes.

6. Preheat oven to 400°F. Fill a large Dutch oven ¾ full with water. Bring to a boil over high heat. Add baking soda. Carefully drop pretzels, 3 at a time, into boiling water for 10 seconds. Remove with slotted spoon. Place on parchment-lined or well-greased baking sheets. Sprinkle with coarse salt, sesame seeds or poppy seeds.

7. Bake 15 minutes or until golden brown. Place on wire rack. *Makes 18 large pretzels*

Caramel-Cinnamon Snack Mix

2 tablespoons vegetable oil
½ cup popcorn kernels
½ teaspoon salt, divided
1½ cups packed light brown sugar
½ cup butter or margarine
½ cup corn syrup
¼ cup red hot cinnamon candies
2 cups cinnamon-flavored shaped graham crackers
1 cup red and green candy coated chocolate pieces

1. Grease 2 large baking pans; set aside.

2. Heat oil in large saucepan over high heat until hot. Add corn kernels. Cover pan. Shake pan constantly over heat until kernels no longer pop. Divide popcorn evenly between 2 large bowls. Add ¼ teaspoon salt to each bowl; toss to coat. Set aside.

3. Preheat oven to 250°F. Combine sugar, butter and corn syrup in heavy, medium saucepan. Cook over medium heat until sugar melts, stirring constantly with wooden spoon. Bring mixture to a boil. Boil 5 minutes, stirring frequently.

4. Remove ½ of sugar mixture (about ¾ cup) from saucepan; pour over 1 portion of popcorn. Toss with lightly greased spatula until evenly coated.

5. Add red hot candies to saucepan. Stir constantly with wooden spoon until melted. Pour over remaining portion of popcorn; toss with lightly greased spatula until evenly coated.

6. Spread each portion of popcorn in even layer in separate prepared pans with lightly greased spatula.

7. Bake 1 hour stirring every 15 minutes with wooden spoon to prevent popcorn from sticking together. Cool completely in pans. Combine popcorn, graham crackers and chocolate pieces in large bowl. Store in airtight container at room temperature up to 1 week.

Makes about 4 quarts

Crispy Ranch Breadsticks

2 tablespoons dry ranch party dip mix
2 tablespoons sour cream
I package (10 ounces) refrigerated pizza dough
Butter, melted

1. Preheat oven to 400°F. Combine dip mix and sour cream in small bowl; set aside.

2. Unroll pizza dough on lightly floured work surface. Shape dough into 16×10-inch rectangle. Brush with melted butter. Spread dip mixture evenly over top of dough; cut into 24 (10-inch) strips. Shape into desired shapes.

3. Place breadsticks, ½ inch apart, on parchment-lined or well-greased baking sheets. Bake 10 minutes or until golden brown. Serve immediately or place on wire rack to cool.

Makes 24 breadsticks

Crispy Spiced Nut Breadsticks:
Place I cup chopped pecans and I tablespoon vegetable oil in plastic bag; toss to coat. Combine ¼ teaspoon chili powder, ¼ teaspoon ground cumin, ¼ teaspoon curry powder, ⅛ teaspoon ground cinnamon and a dash of ground red pepper in small bowl. Add to nuts; toss to coat. Place nuts in small pan over medium heat and stir constantly until nuts are lightly toasted. Sprinkle nut mixture with I teaspoon garlic salt; cool to room temperature. Instead of spreading dough with sour cream mixture, sprinkle ½ cup very finely chopped spiced nuts over dough (store remaining nuts in tightly covered container). Cut into 24 (10-inch) strips. Shape into desired shapes. Bake as directed.

Top to bottom: Crispy Spiced Nut Breadsticks and Crispy Ranch Breadsticks

Santa Fe Trail Mix

1½ cups pecan halves
1 cup cashews
¾ cup roasted shelled
   pistachio nuts
½ cup pine nuts
⅓ cup roasted sunflower
   seeds
3 tablespoons butter
2½ teaspoons ground cumin
¼ teaspoon garlic powder
¼ cup plus 1 tablespoon
   chili sauce
1 chipotle chile in adobo
   sauce, about 3 inches
   long
1 tablespoon frozen orange
   juice concentrate,
   thawed
   Cooking spray
1 tablespoon dried cilantro,
   divided

1. Preheat oven to 300°F. Line 14×11-inch baking sheet with foil; set aside.

2. Combine pecans, cashews, pistachios, pine nuts and sunflower seeds in large bowl.

3. Combine butter, cumin and garlic powder in small microwavable bowl. Microwave on HIGH 45 to 50 seconds or until butter is melted and foamy; stir to blend.

4. Place butter mixture, chili sauce, chipotle chile and orange juice concentrate in food processor or blender; process until smooth. Pour sauce over nut mixture; stir to coat evenly. Spread mixture in single layer on prepared baking sheet.

5. Bake about 1 hour, stirring every 10 minutes. Remove from oven and spray mixture evenly with cooking spray. Crush dried cilantro between fingers and sprinkle 1½ teaspoons over mixture. Stir mixture with spatula and repeat with additional cooking spray and remaining cilantro. Set baking sheet on wire rack to cool. Leave uncovered at least 1 hour before storing in airtight container or resealable plastic food storage bag.

Makes 4 cups

Antipasto Crescent Bites

2 ounces cream cheese (do not use reduced fat or fat-free cream cheese)
1 package (8 ounces) refrigerated crescent roll dough
1 egg *plus* 1 tablespoon water, beaten
4 strips roasted red pepper, cut into ¾×3-inch-long strips
2 large marinated artichoke hearts, cut in half lengthwise to ¾ inch width
1 thin slice Genoa or other salami, cut into 4 strips
4 small stuffed olives, cut in half

1. Preheat oven to 375°F. Cut cream cheese into 16 equal pieces, about 1 teaspoon per piece; set aside.

2. Remove dough from package. Unroll on lightly floured surface. Cut each triangle of dough in half to form 2 triangles. Brush outer edges of triangle lightly with beaten egg.

3. Wrap 1 pepper strip around 1 piece of cream cheese. Place on dough triangle. Fold over and pinch edges to seal; repeat with remaining pepper strips. Place 1 piece artichoke heart and 1 piece of cream cheese on dough triangle. Fold over and pinch edges to seal; repeat with remaining artichoke hearts. Wrap 1 strip salami around 1 piece of cream cheese. Place on dough triangle. Fold over and pinch edges to seal; repeat with remaining salami. Place 2 olive halves and 1 piece of cream cheese on dough triangle. Fold over and pinch edges to seal; repeat with remaining olives. Place evenly spaced on ungreased baking sheet. Brush with beaten egg.

4. Bake 12 to 14 minutes, or until golden brown. Cool on wire rack. Store in airtight container in refrigerator.

5. Reheat on baking sheet in preheated 325°F oven 7 to 8 minutes or until warmed through. Do not microwave.

Makes 16 pieces

Sun-Dried Tomato Pizza Snack Mix

2 cups wheat cereal squares
2 cups unsweetened puffed corn cereal
2 cups puffed rice cereal
2 cups square mini cheese crackers
1 cup roasted sunflower seeds
3 tablespoons grated Parmesan cheese
3 tablespoons butter
2 tablespoons olive oil
2 teaspoons dried Italian seasoning
1½ teaspoons garlic powder
¼ cup tomato sauce
1 teaspoon balsamic vinegar
⅜ teaspoon sugar
⅛ teaspoon salt
8 to 9 sun-dried tomatoes packed in oil, diced

1. Preheat oven to 250°F. Spray 13×9-inch baking pan with nonstick cooking spray.

2. Combine cereal squares, puffed corn, puffed rice, cheese crackers and sunflower seeds in large bowl; set aside.

3. Combine cheese, butter, oil, Italian seasoning and garlic powder in medium bowl. Microwave on HIGH 1 to 1½ minutes until foamy and herbs release their aromas. Stir in tomato sauce, vinegar, sugar and salt. Pour over cereal mixture; stir well to coat. Place in prepared pan and spread to one layer.

4. Bake 55 to 60 minutes, stirring every 15 minutes. Stir in sun-dried tomatoes 15 minutes before finished baking. Let cool in pan set on wire rack about 2 hours, leaving uncovered until mixture is crisp and tomato pieces have lost their moisture. Store in airtight container or resealable plastic food storage bag. *Makes 7 cups*

Sun-Dried Tomato Pizza Snack Mix

Chocolate Biscotti Nuggets

¾ cup old-fashioned or
     quick oats
2¼ cups all-purpose flour
1½ teaspoons baking
     powder
½ teaspoon salt
¾ cup chopped dates
½ cup coarsely chopped
     toasted pecans
½ cup honey
2 large eggs
1 teaspoon vanilla
½ cup (1 stick), butter
     melted
   Grated peel of 2 oranges

CHOCOLATE COATING
1¾ cups semisweet dark
     chocolate or white
     chocolate chips
4 teaspoons shortening

1. Grease baking sheet; set aside. Preheat oven to 350°F.

2. Place oats in food processor; process until oats resemble coarse flour. Combine oats, flour, baking powder and salt in large bowl. Stir in dates and pecans.

3. Whisk together honey, eggs and vanilla in medium bowl. Add melted butter and orange peel. Stir egg mixture into oat mixture just until blended. Turn out dough onto lightly floured surface; flatten slightly. Knead until dough holds together, adding flour if necessary to prevent sticking. Divide dough into 3 equal pieces; roll each into 9×½-inch log. Carefully transfer logs to prepared baking sheet, spacing about 2 inches apart. If dough cracks, pat back into shape.

4. Bake logs 25 to 30 minutes or until lightly golden but still soft. Remove from oven. *Reduce oven temperature to 275°F.* Let logs cool on baking sheet 10 minutes. Trim ends using serrated knife. Slice logs on slight diagonal about ¾ inch thick. Arrange biscotti on their sides on baking sheet. Return to oven and bake 15 to 20 minutes or until lightly golden. Turn biscotti over and bake 10 to 15 minutes longer. Remove biscotti to wire rack to cool completely.

5. Brush individual biscotti with dry pastry brush to remove any loose crumbs. Heat chocolate chips and shortening in small heavy saucepan over very low heat until melted and smooth. Dip half of each biscotti slice into melted chocolate, letting any excess run off. Place on prepared baking sheet. Let stand until set. Store in waxed paper-lined tin at room temperature.

Makes about 36 biscotti slices

Dress It Up with Condiments

Homestyle Mixed Berry Freezer Jam

  1 package (16 ounces) frozen mixed
      berries, thawed
3¾ cups sugar
  2 teaspoons grated orange peel (optional)
  1 pouch (3 ounces) liquid pectin
  2 tablespoons orange juice

1. Place berries in food processor or blender; process until pieces are about ¼ inch in size. Combine berries, sugar and orange peel in large bowl; stir 2 minutes. Let stand 10 minutes.

2. Combine pectin and orange juice in small bowl; stir into berry mixture. Stir 2 minutes to blend thoroughly. Spoon into 4 labeled 1-cup freezer containers, leaving ½-inch space at top of container. Cover with tight-fitting lids. Let stand 24 hours to set. Refrigerate up to 3 weeks or freeze up to 6 months.

Makes 4 (1-cup) containers

Left to right: Homestyle Mixed Berry Freezer Jam and Cranberry-Peach Freezer Jam (page 26)

Cranberry-Peach Freezer Jam

3 cups (12 ounces) fresh or
   frozen cranberries,
   thawed
2 cups coarsely chopped
   fresh peaches
6 cups sugar
¾ cup peach nectar
1 teaspoon grated fresh
   ginger (optional)
2 pouches (3 ounces each)
   liquid pectin
¼ cup lemon juice

1. Place cranberries in food
processor or blender; process
until pieces are ⅛ inch in size.
Transfer to large bowl. Place
peaches in food processor or
blender; process until pieces are
¼ inch in size. Add peaches,
sugar, peach nectar and ginger to
cranberries; stir 2 minutes. Let
stand 10 minutes.

2. Combine pectin and lemon
juice in small bowl; stir into fruit
mixture. Stir 2 minutes to mix
thoroughly.

3. Spoon into 7 labeled 1-cup
freezer containers, leaving
½-inch space at top. Cover with
tight-fitting lids. Let stand 24
hours to set. Refrigerate up to 3
weeks or freeze up to 6 months.
   Makes 7 (1-cup) containers

Champagne-Strawberry Freezer Jam

4 cups fresh strawberries
   (about 2 pints)
1½ cups champagne
3 cups sugar
1 box (1.75 ounces) fruit
   pectin for lower sugar
   recipes

1. Place strawberries in food
processor or blender; process
until pieces are about ¼ inch in
size. Measure 3¼ cups; set aside.

2. Bring champagne to a boil
over high heat in medium
saucepan. Reduce heat to
medium-low; simmer 5 minutes.
Remove from heat; let stand 15
minutes. Return champagne to
2-cup measuring cup; add
enough water to equal 1 cup.

3. Combine sugar and pectin in
medium bowl; blend well.
Combine sugar mixture and
champagne in large saucepan.
Bring to a boil over medium-
high heat, stirring constantly.
Continue boiling 1 minute
longer, stirring constantly.
Remove from heat. Add
strawberries; stir 1 minute.

4. Spoon into 5 labeled 1-cup freezer containers, leaving ½-inch space at top of container. Cover with tight-fitting lids. Let stand at room temperature 24 hours to set. Refrigerate up to 3 weeks or freeze up to 6 months.

Makes 5 (1-cup) containers

Almond-Cranberry Syrup

1 package (12 ounces) frozen cranberries, thawed
1 cup sugar
¾ cup corn syrup
¼ teaspoon almond extract (optional)

1. Combine cranberries and ¼ cup water in medium saucepan. Bring to a boil over high heat. Boil 10 minutes or until cranberries are tender and pop, stirring frequently with wooden spoon.

2. Add sugar and corn syrup to saucepan. Bring to a boil over high heat. Boil 10 minutes or until mixture thickens and coats wooden spoon, stirring constantly. Remove saucepan from heat.

3. Place wire mesh sieve over medium bowl. Pour cranberry mixture into sieve, pressing cranberries with back of wooden spoon to extract all of juices. Add almond extract. Cool completely. Reserve cranberries for another use.*

4. When syrup has cooled completely, strain again in wire mesh sieve; discard solids.

5. To transfer syrup to clean, dry decorative glass bottle, place neck of funnel in bottle. Pour syrup into funnel. Remove funnel; seal bottle. Store in airtight container in refrigerator up to 2 months.

Makes about 1¾ cups

Spoon cranberries into clean, dry decorative jar; cover. Serve as a spread.

Cracked Peppercorn Honey Mustard

2½ cups Dijon mustard
1 jar (9.5 ounces) extra grainy Dijon mustard
¾ cup honey
2 tablespoons cracked black pepper
1 tablespoon dried tarragon leaves (optional)

1. Combine Dijon mustard, grainy Dijon mustard, honey, pepper and tarragon in medium bowl. Blend with wire whisk.

2. Spoon into 4 labeled 1¼-cup containers. Store refrigerated up to 4 weeks.

Makes 4 (1¼-cup) containers

Asian Spicy Sweet Mustard

1 jar (16 ounces) spicy brown mustard
1 cup peanut butter
¾ cup hoisin sauce
½ cup packed brown sugar

1. Combine mustard, peanut butter, hoisin sauce and sugar in medium bowl. Blend with wire whisk.

2. Spoon into 4 labeled 1-cup containers. Store refrigerated up to 4 weeks.

Makes 4 (1-cup) containers

HELPFUL HINTS

Create your own snack-attack gift bag. Fill a holiday gift bag with colorful tissue paper, a jar of Cracked Peppercorn Honey Mustard, a jar of Asian Spicy Sweet Mustard and a tin of Soft Pretzels (page 10) for the ideal homespun gift for all your neighbors.

Left to right: Cracked Peppercorn Honey Mustard and Asian Spicy Sweet Mustard

Texas Hot & Tangy BBQ Sauce

¼ cup vegetable oil
2 cups finely chopped onion
6 cloves garlic, minced
2 cups water
1 can (12 ounces) tomato paste
1 cup packed brown sugar
¾ cup apple cider vinegar
½ cup molasses
¼ cup **Worcestershire** sauce
2 tablespoons jalapeño pepper sauce
2 teaspoons chili powder
2 teaspoons ground cumin
½ teaspoon ground red pepper

1. Heat oil in large skillet over medium-high heat 1 minute. Add onion; cook and stir 8 to 10 minutes or until onion begins to brown. Add garlic; cook 2 minutes longer or until onion is golden. Add water, tomato paste, sugar, vinegar, molasses, Worcestershire sauce, jalapeño pepper sauce, chili powder, cumin and ground red pepper. Stir with wire whisk until well blended. Reduce heat to medium-low; simmer 15 minutes, stirring occasionally. Cover and remove from heat. Cool 30 minutes.

2. Spoon into 4 labeled 12-ounce containers. Store refrigerated up to 3 weeks.

Makes 5 to 5½ cups

HELPFUL HINTS

Take the chill out of winter with a summer-theme gift basket. Pack a picnic basket with a tablecloth, a festive jar filled with Texas Hot & Tangy BBQ Sauce, a loaf of crusty bread and a nice bottle of wine. A picnic by the fire is just the gift for the outdoors fanatic in your family.

Citrus-Plum Barbecue Sauce

2 containers (12 ounces each) orange juice concentrate
2 jars (12 ounces each) plum preserves
½ cup honey
½ cup tomato paste
¼ cup dry sherry
2 tablespoons minced ginger
2 tablespoons soy sauce
2 cloves garlic, minced
½ teaspoon salt
½ teaspoon black pepper

1. Combine orange juice concentrate, plum preserves, honey, tomato paste, sherry, ginger, soy sauce, garlic, salt and pepper in large saucepan. Heat over medium-high heat until mixture begins to simmer. Reduce heat to medium-low; simmer 10 minutes. Cover and remove from heat. Cool 30 minutes.

2. Spoon into 4 labeled 12-ounce containers. Store refrigerated up to 3 weeks.

Makes 5½ to 6 cups

Citrus-Plum Barbecue Sauce

Rio Grande Salsa

1 **canned chipotle chili pepper, 1 teaspoon adobo sauce reserved***
1 **tablespoon vegetable oil**
1 **onion, chopped**
3 **cloves garlic, minced**
2 **teaspoons ground cumin**
1½ **teaspoons chili powder**
2 **cans (14½ ounces each) diced tomatoes, drained**
½ **cup chopped fresh cilantro leaves**
¾ **teaspoon sugar**
½ **teaspoon salt**

Chipotle chili peppers are smoked jalapeño peppers and are commonly available canned in adobo sauce.

1. To seed chipotle chili, slit chili open lengthwise with scissors or knife. Carefully pull out and discard seeds and veins. Cut into slices. Hold slices together and finely chop. (Chipotle chili peppers can sting and irritate the skin; wear rubber gloves when handling peppers and do not touch eyes. Wash hands after handling chili peppers.)

2. Heat oil in medium saucepan over medium-high heat until hot. Add onion and garlic. Cook and stir 5 minutes or until onion is tender. Add cumin and chili powder; cook 30 seconds, stirring frequently. Add chili with adobo sauce and tomatoes. Reduce heat to medium-low. Simmer 10 to 12 minutes or until salsa is thickened, stirring occasionally.

3. Remove saucepan from heat; stir in cilantro, sugar and salt. Cool completely. Store in airtight container in refrigerator up to 3 weeks.

Makes about 3 cups

Note: *This salsa is very spicy. For a milder version, use 1 teaspoon chopped chipotle chili pepper.*

Pineapple-Peach Salsa

2 cans (20 ounces each) pineapple tidbits in juice, drained
2 cans (15 ounces each) peach slices in juice, drained and chopped
1 can (15 ounces) black beans, rinsed and drained
¼ cup finely chopped red bell pepper
2 jalapeño peppers,* seeded and chopped
2 tablespoons chopped fresh cilantro
2 tablespoons lime juice
2 tablespoons red wine vinegar
½ teaspoon salt
¼ teaspoon ground red pepper
¼ teaspoon garlic powder

*Jalapeño peppers can sting and irritate the skin; wear rubber gloves when handling peppers and do not touch eyes.

1. Combine pineapple, peaches, beans, red bell pepper, jalapeño peppers, cilantro, lime juice, vinegar, salt, ground red pepper and garlic powder in large bowl; toss to coat.

2. Spoon into 4 labeled 1¾-cup containers. Store in containers in refrigerator up to 2 weeks.

Makes 4 (1¾-cup) containers

TIP: This tropical salsa bursting with fresh flavor is great served with chicken, fish or pork.

Roasted Pepper & Tomato Salsa

3 yellow or red bell peppers
2 poblano peppers
1 large onion
4 cloves garlic, minced
2 tablespoons olive oil
1 teaspoon dried oregano
¾ teaspoon salt
½ teaspoon black pepper
2 cans diced tomatoes
¾ cup tomato juice
¼ cup chopped fresh
   cilantro
1 tablespoon lime juice

1. Preheat oven to 350°F. Chop peppers and onion into ¾-inch pieces. Combine peppers, onion, garlic, olive oil, oregano, salt and black pepper in large bowl; toss to coat. Spread onto two 15×10×1-inch baking pans. Bake 20 minutes or until peppers and onion are lightly browned, stirring after 10 minutes.

2. Combine roasted vegetables and remaining ingredients in large bowl. Spoon into 4 labeled 1½-cup storage containers. Store in refrigerator up to 10 days or freeze up to 2 months.
Makes 4 (1½-cup) containers

Roasted Pepper & Tomato Salsa

Gingered Apple-Cranberry Chutney

**2 medium Granny Smith
apples, peeled and
chopped**
**1 package (12 ounces) fresh
or thawed frozen
cranberries**
**1¼ cups packed light brown
sugar**
**¾ cup cranberry juice
cocktail**
½ cup golden raisins
**¼ cup chopped
crystallized ginger**
¼ cup cider vinegar
**1 teaspoon ground
cinnamon**
⅛ teaspoon ground allspice

1. Combine apples, cranberries, sugar, cranberry juice cocktail, raisins, ginger, vinegar, cinnamon and allspice in heavy, medium saucepan.

2. Bring to a boil over high heat. Reduce heat to medium. Simmer 20 minutes or until mixture is very thick, stirring occasionally with wooden spoon.

3. Remove saucepan from heat. Cool completely. Store in airtight container in refrigerator up to 2 weeks.

Makes about 3 cups

Chocolate-Cherry Chutney

2 jars (16 ounces each) maraschino cherries
8 ounces semisweet chocolate, coarsely chopped
1 can (5 ounces) evaporated milk
1 cup powdered sugar
1½ cups slivered or chopped toasted almonds
1 cup white chocolate chips

1. Drain cherries, reserving ¼ cup juice. Coarsely chop cherries; set aside.

2. Melt chocolate and evaporated milk in microwave on HIGH 3 to 4 minutes or until melted, stirring after 2 minutes. Add powdered sugar and reserved juice. Microwave 1 minute; stir until smooth. Stir in chopped cherries, toasted almonds and white chocolate chips.

3. Spoon into 4 labeled 1¼-cup containers. Store refrigerated up to 4 weeks.

Makes 4 (1¼-cup) containers

TIP: This chunky chocolatey treat is fabulous served with ice cream, cake, cookies or other desserts.

Carrot-Walnut Chutney

1 pound fresh carrots, peeled and chopped into ½-inch pieces
2 tablespoons vegetable oil
1½ cups chopped onions
¾ cup packed brown sugar
¼ cup apple cider vinegar
1 teaspoon ground allspice
1 teaspoon ground cumin
½ teaspoon black pepper
½ teaspoon ground cinnamon
¼ teaspoon salt
1 cup raisins
1½ cups chopped toasted walnuts

1. Place carrots and ⅓ cup water in large saucepan; cover. Bring to a boil over high heat; reduce heat to low. Simmer 8 to 10 minutes or until tender; drain.

2. Heat oil in large skillet over medium-high heat 1 minute. Add onions; cook and stir 6 to 8 minutes or until golden brown. Stir in sugar, vinegar, allspice, cumin, pepper, cinnamon and salt; simmer 1 minute. Add raisins; simmer 3 minutes. Remove from heat; stir in carrots and walnuts. Spoon into 4 labeled 1-cup containers. Store refrigerated up to 4 weeks.

Makes 4 (1-cup) containers

Chocolate-Cherry Chutney

Chunky Fruit Chutney

2 cans (15¼ ounces each) tropical fruit salad packed in light syrup and passion fruit juice
1 can (15 ounces) apricot halves in extra light syrup
1 cup chopped green bell pepper
1 cup chopped red bell pepper
¼ cup packed brown sugar
1 teaspoon curry powder
1 teaspoon onion powder
½ teaspoon salt
½ teaspoon garlic powder
½ teaspoon ground ginger
½ teaspoon red pepper flakes
½ teaspoon coarse ground black pepper

1. Drain tropical fruit salad, reserving ½ cup liquid. Drain apricots; discard syrup. Chop fruit salad and apricots into ½-inch pieces.

2. Combine bell peppers, reserved ½ cup juice, sugar, curry powder, onion powder, salt, garlic powder, ginger, red pepper flakes and black pepper in large skillet. Bring to a boil over high heat. Reduce heat to medium-high; simmer 6 to 8 minutes or until most liquid is evaporated and bell peppers are tender. Remove from heat. Stir in chopped fruit.

3. Spoon into 4 labeled 1¼-cup containers. Store refrigerated up to 4 weeks.
    Makes 4 (1¼-cup) containers

Clockwise from top right: Carrot-Walnut Chutney (page 38) and Chunky Fruit Chutney

Bountiful Bread Basket

Cranberry-Cheese Batter Bread

- 1¼ cups milk
- 3 cups all-purpose flour
- ½ cup sugar
- 1 package active dry yeast
- 1 teaspoon salt
- ½ cup (1 stick) butter, chilled
- ½ cup (4 ounces) cream cheese, chilled
- 1 cup (3-ounce package) dried cranberries

1. Heat milk in small saucepan over low heat until temperature reaches 120° to 130°F. Grease 8-inch square pan; set aside. Combine flour, sugar, yeast and salt in large bowl.

2. Cut butter and cream cheese into 1-inch chunks; add to flour mixture. Cut in butter and cream cheese with pastry blender until mixture resembles course crumbs. Add cranberries; toss. Add warm milk; beat 1 minute or until dough looks stringy. Place batter in prepared pan. Cover with towel; let rise in warm place about 1 hour.

3. Preheat oven to 375°F. Bake 35 minutes or until golden brown.   *Makes 1 loaf*

Walnut-Chocolate Quick Bread

1½ cups milk
1 cup sugar
⅓ cup vegetable oil
1 egg, beaten
1 tablespoon molasses
1 teaspoon vanilla
3 cups all-purpose flour
3 tablespoons unsweetened
   cocoa powder
2 teaspoons baking soda
2 teaspoons baking powder
1 teaspoon salt
1 cup chocolate chips
½ cup walnuts, coarsely
   chopped

1. Preheat oven to 350°F. Grease four 5×3-inch loaf pans; set aside.

2. Combine milk, sugar, oil, egg, molasses and vanilla in medium bowl. Stir until sugar is dissolved; set aside.

3. Whisk together flour, cocoa, baking soda, baking powder and salt in large bowl. Add chocolate chips, nuts and sugar mixture; stir just until combined. Pour into prepared pans.

4. Bake 30 minutes or until toothpick inserted near center of loaf comes out clean. Cool in pan 15 minutes. Remove from pan and cool on wire rack.

Makes 4 loaves

Muffin Variation: *Preheat oven to 375°F. Spoon batter into 12 greased muffin cups. Bake 20 minutes or until toothpick inserted near center of muffin comes out clean.*

HELPFUL HINTS

Create a chocolate-lover's-delight gift basket. Begin by lining a basket with a beautiful cloth napkin. Arrange a loaf of Walnut-Chocolate Quick Bread wrapped in clear plastic wrap and tied with a gold ribbon, a decorative tin filled with Black Russian Truffles (page 92) and a jar of Chocolate-Cherry Chutney (page 38) in the basket. To add the final touch, sprinkle with individually wrapped Black and White Caramels (page 78). Voila! The perfect elegant gift for any chocoholic.

Tex-Mex Quick Bread

1½ **cups all-purpose flour**
  1 **cup Monterey Jack cheese**
  ½ **cup cornmeal**
  ½ **cup sun-dried tomatoes,
    coarsely chopped**
  1 **can (4.25 ounces) black
    olives, drained and
    chopped**
  ¼ **cup sugar**
1½ **teaspoons baking
    powder**
  1 **teaspoon baking soda**
  1 **cup milk**
  1 **can (4.5 ounces) green
    chilies, drained and
    chopped**
  ¼ **cup olive oil**
  1 **large egg, beaten**

1. Preheat oven to 325°F. Grease
9×5-inch loaf pan or four 5×3-
inch loaf pans; set aside.

2. Combine flour, cheese,
cornmeal, tomatoes, olives, sugar,
baking powder and baking soda
in large bowl.

3. Combine milk, chilies, oil and
egg in small bowl. Add to flour
mixture; stir just until combined.
Pour into prepared pan. Bake
9×5-inch loaf 45 minutes and
5×3-inch loaves 30 minutes or
until toothpick inserted near
center of loaf comes out clean.
Cool in pan 15 minutes. Remove
from pan and cool on wire rack.

*Makes 1 large loaf or
4 small loaves*

Muffin Variation: *Preheat oven to
375°F. Spoon batter into 12 well-
greased muffin cups. Bake 20
minutes or until toothpick inserted
near center of muffin comes out
clean.*

Basic Yeast Bread

2 cups milk
¼ cup unsalted butter,
softened
6½ to 7½ cups all-purpose
flour, divided
2 packages active dry yeast
2 teaspoons salt
¼ cup sugar
2 eggs

1. Heat milk and butter in small saucepan over medium heat just until butter is melted. Remove from heat; cool to about 120° to 130°F. Grease two 9×5-inch loaf pans; set aside.

2. Combine 4 cups flour, yeast, salt and sugar in large bowl. Add milk mixture and eggs. Beat vigorously 2 minutes. Add remaining flour, ¼ cup at a time, until dough begins to pull away from sides of bowl.

3. Turn out dough onto lightly floured work surface; flatten slightly. Knead 10 minutes or until smooth and elastic, adding flour if necessary to prevent sticking.

4. Shape dough into a ball. Place in large lightly oiled bowl; turn dough over once to oil surface. Cover with towel; let rise in warm place about 1 hour or until doubled in bulk.

5. Turn out dough onto lightly oiled work surface; divide in half. Shape each half of dough into loaf; place in prepared pans. Cover with towel; let rise in warm place 45 minutes.

6. Preheat oven to 375°F. Bake 25 minutes or until loaves are golden and sound hollow when tapped. Immediately remove bread from pans and cool on wire rack.   *Makes 2 loaves*

Hot Cross Buns

Basic Yeast Bread (page 48)
2 cups raisins
½ cup powdered sugar
2 to 4 tablespoons heavy
cream

1. Prepare Basic Yeast Bread through Step 4. Grease two 13×9-inch pans. Turn out dough onto lightly oiled surface; divide in half. Keep remaining half covered. Knead 1 cup raisins into half of dough. Cover with towel; let rest 5 minutes.

2. Divide dough into 15 equal pieces. Form each piece into ball. Place evenly spaced in prepared pan. Cover with towel; let rise in warm place 45 minutes. Repeat with remaining dough. Preheat oven to 400°F. Bake 15 minutes or until golden brown. Immediately remove from pan; cool on wire rack 30 minutes. Combine powdered sugar and cream, 2 tablespoons at a time, in measuring cup. Add additional cream to reach desired consistency. Pour mixture in thin stream across each bun to form a cross. *Makes 30 buns*

Hot Cross Buns

Cheddar Pepper Bread

Basic Yeast Bread (page 48)
⅔ **cup chopped red bell pepper**
⅔ **cup chopped green bell pepper**
½ **cup chopped onion**
2 **cups cubed sharp Cheddar cheese**
2 **eggs**
Coarse salt (optional)

1. Prepare Basic Yeast Bread through Step 4. Grease baking sheets; set aside. Turn out dough onto lightly oiled work surface; divide in half.

2. Combine bell peppers, onion and cheese in medium bowl; divide in half. Knead half the pepper mixture into half the dough. Knead the other half of pepper mixture into other half of dough. Cover with towel on work surface; let rest 5 minutes.

3. Round each half of dough into a ball. Place on prepared baking sheets. Flatten each round of dough to about 2 inches thick. Cover with towel; let rise in warm place 45 minutes.

4. Beat eggs with 2 tablespoons water in small bowl. Lightly brush tops and sides of each loaf with egg mixture. Sprinkle tops of loaves with coarse salt, if desired.

5. Preheat oven to 375°F. Bake 30 minutes or until golden brown. Immediately remove loaves from baking sheets and allow to cool on wire rack.

Makes 2 loaves

Chocolate Rolls

Basic Yeast Bread (page 48)
1 cup granulated sugar
6 tablespoons unsweetened
    cocoa powder, divided
1 teaspoon ground
    cinnamon
6 tablespoons butter, melted
2 cups powdered sugar
1/2 to 3/4 cup heavy cream

1. Prepare Basic Yeast Bread through Step 4. Grease two 13×9×2-inch pans; set aside. Turn out dough onto lightly oiled work surface; divide in half. Roll half the dough into 20×15-inch rectangle.

2. Combine granulated sugar, 4 tablespoons cocoa and cinnamon in small bowl.

3. Brush melted butter over dough, leaving 1/2-inch border on top short edge. Sprinkle half the sugar mixture over dough. Starting at short side; loosely roll up dough jelly-roll style. Using heavy thread or dental floss, cut dough in 12 equal slices. Place slices, cut side up, in prepared pan. Cover with towel; let rise 45 minutes. Repeat with remaining half of dough.

4. Preheat oven to 375°F. Bake 20 minutes or until golden brown. Allow rolls to cool in pan 30 minutes.

5. Combine powdered sugar, 2 tablespoons cocoa and 4 tablespoons cream in glass measuring cup. Add additional cream if necessary to reach desired consistency. Drizzle over tops of rolls.   *Makes 24 rolls*

Savory Pull-Apart Loaves

Basic Yeast Bread (page 48)
2 tablespoons dried basil
2 tablespoons rubbed sage
2 tablespoons dried thyme
2 tablespoons olive oil

1. Prepare Basic Yeast Bread through Step 4. Grease two 9×5-inch loaf pans; set aside. Combine basil, sage and thyme in small bowl; set aside.

2. Divide half the dough into 16 equal pieces. Keep remaining half of dough covered. Form each piece into a ball. Cover with towel on work surface; let rest 5 minutes.

3. Flatten each ball into 4×3-inch oval. Coat both sides of dough with olive oil. Sprinkle one side of dough with rounded ½ teaspoon of herb mixture.

4. Stand loaf pan on short end. Lay one piece of dough, herb-covered side down, in pan. Stack remaining 15 pieces of dough in pan so that herb-covered sides of dough are touching sides of dough not covered with herb mixture. Cover with towel; let rise 45 minutes. Repeat with remaining half of dough.

5. Preheat oven to 375°F. Bake 35 minutes or until tops of loaves are golden. Immediately remove bread from pan and cool on wire rack.   *Makes 2 loaves*

Greek Flat Breads

Basic Yeast Bread (page 48)
1 cup chopped kalamata olives
6 cloves garlic, minced
½ pound crumbled feta cheese
2 tablespoons olive oil
2 eggs
Coarse salt (optional)

1. Prepare Basic Yeast Bread through Step 4. Grease 2 baking sheets; set aside. Turn out dough onto lightly oiled work surface; divide in half. Keep remaining half of dough covered. Divide dough into 16 equal pieces. Form each piece into ball. Cover with towel on work surface; let rest 5 minutes.

2. Combine olives, garlic, cheese and oil in medium bowl; set aside.

3. Beat eggs with 2 tablespoons water in small bowl.

4. Flatten each ball of dough to ½ inch thick. Place 2 inches apart on prepared baking sheet. Brush dough with beaten egg. Divide half the olive mixture into 16 equal portions. Sprinkle each round of dough with 1 portion of olive mixture; press topping into dough slightly.

5. Cover with towel; let rise 45 minutes. Repeat with remaining half of dough.

6. Place heavy pan on lower rack of oven. Preheat oven to 400°F.

7. Sprinkle tops of dough with coarse salt, if desired. Place bread in oven. Carefully place 4 to 5 ice cubes in heavy pan; close door immediately. Bake 15 minutes or until lightly browned. Immediately remove bread from baking sheets and place on wire rack to cool.

Makes 32 flat breads

Festive Caramel Floral Rolls

2 cups water
1 cup firmly packed dark brown sugar, divided
½ cup vegetable shortening
5½ to 6 cups all-purpose flour, divided
2 packages active dry yeast
2 teaspoons salt
2 teaspoons baking powder
2 teaspoons vanilla
3 tablespoons butter
3 tablespoons milk

1. Heat water, ½ cup brown sugar and shortening in small saucepan over medium heat until sugar is dissolved and shortening is melted. Remove from heat; cool to 120° to 130°F.

2. Combine 3 cups flour, yeast, salt and baking powder in large bowl. Add water mixture and vanilla; beat vigorously 2 minutes. Add remaining flour, ¼ cup at a time, until dough begins to pull away from sides of bowl. Turn out dough onto floured work surface; flatten slightly. Knead 10 minutes or until smooth and elastic, adding flour if necessary to prevent sticking.

3. Shape dough into a ball. Place in large lightly oiled bowl; turn dough over once to oil surface. Cover with towel; let rise in warm place about 1 hour or until doubled in bulk.

4. Turn dough out onto lightly oiled work surface. Divide into 24 equal pieces. Form each piece into ball. Cover with towel on work surface; let rest 5 minutes.

5. Roll 12 balls of dough into 10-inch ropes. Keep remaining balls covered. Tie one 10-inch rope into knot. Place in center of lightly oiled baking sheet. Form remaining 11 ropes into tear drop shape so loose ends touch. Place on baking sheet around dough knot to form daisy-like flower. Repeat with remaining dough.

6. Preheat oven to 375°F. Bake 25 minutes or until deep golden brown.

7. While bread is baking, melt butter in small saucepan over medium-low heat. When butter begins to bubble, add remaining ½ cup brown sugar; stir 3 minutes. Add milk. Bring to a boil without stirring. Cook 3 minutes; remove from heat and cool.

8. When bread is done baking, immediately remove bread from baking sheet and cool on wire rack. Brush each loaf with butter mixture using pastry brush.

Makes 2 loaves

Festive Caramel Floral Roll

Sage Buns

1 1/2 **cups milk**
  2 **tablespoons vegetable shortening**
  3 **to 4 cups all-purpose flour, divided**
  2 **tablespoons sugar**
  1 **package active dry yeast**
  2 **teaspoons rubbed sage**
  1 **teaspoon salt**
  1 **tablespoon olive oil (optional)**

1. Heat milk and shortening in small saucepan over medium heat, stirring constantly, until shortening is melted and temperature reaches 120° to 130°F. Remove from heat. Grease 13×9-inch pan; set aside.

2. Combine 2 cups flour, sugar, yeast, sage and salt in large bowl. Add milk mixture; beat vigorously 2 minutes. Add remaining flour, 1/4 cup at a time, until dough begins to pull away from sides of bowl.

3. Turn out dough onto floured work surface; flatten slightly. Knead 10 minutes or until dough is smooth and elastic, adding flour if necessary to prevent sticking.

4. Shape dough into ball. Place in large lightly oiled bowl; turn dough over once to oil surface. Cover with towel; let rise in warm place 1 hour or until doubled in bulk.

5. Turn out dough onto lightly oiled surface. Divide into 24 equal pieces. Form each piece into ball. Place evenly spaced in prepared pan. Cover with towel; let rise 45 minutes.

6. Preheat oven to 375°F. Bake 15 to 20 minutes or until golden brown. Immediately remove bread from pan and cool on wire rack. Brush tops of rolls with olive oil for a soft shiny top, if desired. *Makes 24 rolls*

Maple-Pumpkin-Pecan Twist

1 can (15 ounces) pumpkin
1 cup water
½ cup vegetable shortening
7 to 8 cups all-purpose flour, divided
2 cups pecans, coarsely chopped
½ cup sugar
2 packages active dry yeast
2 teaspoons salt
2 large eggs
2 teaspoons maple flavoring, divided
6 to 8 tablespoons milk
2 cups powdered sugar

1. Heat pumpkin, water and shortening in medium saucepan over medium heat until shortening is melted and temperature reaches 120° to 130°F. Remove from heat.

2. Combine 4 cups flour, pecans, sugar, yeast and salt in large bowl. Add pumpkin mixture, eggs and 1 teaspoon maple flavoring; beat vigorously 2 minutes. Add remaining flour, ¼ cup at a time, until dough begins to pull away from sides of bowl. Turn out dough onto lightly floured work surface; flatten slightly. Knead 10 minutes or until smooth and elastic, adding flour if necessary to prevent sticking. Shape dough into ball. Place in large lightly oiled bowl; turn dough over once to oil surface. Cover with towel; let rise in warm place about 1 hour or until doubled in bulk.

3. Turn out dough onto lightly oiled work surface; divide into four pieces. Shape each piece into 24-inch-long rope. Lightly twist two of the ropes together. Tuck ends under loaf to prevent untwisting. Place on lightly oiled baking sheet. Repeat with remaining two ropes. Cover with towel; let rise in warm place 45 minutes.

4. Preheat oven to 375°F. Bake 25 minutes or until deep golden brown. Immediately remove bread from baking sheets and cool on wire rack 20 minutes.

5. Combine remaining 1 teaspoon maple flavoring and 6 tablespoons milk in small bowl. Whisk milk mixture and powdered sugar together in medium bowl. If icing is too thick, add remaining milk, 1 teaspoon at a time, to reach desired consistency. Drizzle over loaves in zigzag pattern.

Makes 2 large twists

Note: *Twisted ropes can be formed into a ring on baking sheet for an unusual effect.*

Maple-Pumpkin-Pecan Twist

Cookie & Candy Exchange

Rum Fruitcake Cookies

1 cup sugar
¾ cup vegetable shortening
3 large eggs
⅓ cup orange juice
1 tablespoon rum extract
3 cups all-purpose flour
2 teaspoons baking powder
1 teaspoon baking soda
1 teaspoon salt
2 cups (8 ounces) candied fruit
1 cup raisins
1 cup nuts, coarsely chopped

1. Preheat oven to 375°F. Lightly grease cookie sheets; set aside. Beat sugar and shortening in large bowl until fluffy. Add eggs, orange juice and rum extract; beat 2 minutes longer.

2. Combine flour, baking powder, baking soda and salt in small bowl. Add fruit, raisins and nuts. Stir into creamed mixture. Drop dough by rounded teaspoonfuls 2 inches apart onto prepared cookie sheets. Bake 10 to 12 minutes or until golden. Let cookies stand on cookie sheets 2 minutes. Remove to wire rack; cool completely.   *Makes about 6 dozen cookies*

Chocolate Reindeer

**1 cup butter or margarine,
softened**
1 cup sugar
1 egg
1 teaspoon vanilla
**2 ounces semisweet
chocolate, melted**
2¼ cups all-purpose flour
1 teaspoon baking powder
¼ teaspoon salt
Royal Icing (recipe follows)
Assorted small candies

1. Beat butter and sugar in large bowl at high speed of electric mixer until fluffy. Beat in egg and vanilla. Add melted chocolate; mix well. Add flour, baking powder and salt; mix well. Cover and refrigerate about 2 hours or until firm.

2. Preheat oven to 325°F. Grease 2 cookie sheets; set aside.

3. Divide dough in half. Reserve 1 half; wrap remaining dough in plastic wrap and refrigerate.

4. Roll reserved dough on well-floured surface to ¼-inch thickness. Cut with reindeer cookie cutter. Place 2 inches apart on prepared cookie sheet. Chill 10 minutes.

5. Bake 13 to 15 minutes or until set. Cool completely on cookie sheets. Repeat steps with remaining dough.

6. Prepare Royal Icing.

7. To decorate, pipe assorted colored icing on reindeer and add small candies. For best results, let cookies dry overnight uncovered before storing in airtight container at room temperature.

Makes 16 (4-inch) reindeer

ROYAL ICING

2 to 3 large egg whites
2 to 4 cups powdered sugar
1 tablespoon lemon juice

Beat 2 egg whites in medium bowl with electric mixer until peaks just begin to hold their shape. Add 2 cups sugar and lemon juice; beat for 1 minute. If consistency is too thin for piping, gradually add more sugar until desired result is achieved; if it is too thick, add another egg white. Divide icing among several small bowls and tint to desired colors. Keep bowls tightly covered until ready to use.

Date Pinwheel Cookies

1¼ **cups dates, pitted and finely chopped**
¾ **cup orange juice**
½ **cup granulated sugar**
1 **tablespoon butter**
3 **cups plus 1 tablespoon all-purpose flour, divided**
2 **teaspoons vanilla, divided**
4 **ounces cream cheese**
¼ **cup vegetable shortening**
1 **cup packed brown sugar**
2 **eggs**
1 **teaspoon baking soda**
½ **teaspoon salt**

1. Heat dates, orange juice, granulated sugar, butter and 1 tablespoon flour in medium saucepan over medium heat. Cook, stirring frequently 10 minutes or until thick; remove from heat. Stir in 1 teaspoon vanilla; set aside to cool.

2. Beat cream cheese, shortening and brown sugar about 3 minutes in large bowl until light and fluffy. Add eggs and remaining 1 teaspoon vanilla; beat 2 minutes longer.

3. Combine 3 cups flour, baking soda and salt in medium bowl. Add to shortening mixture; stir just until blended. Divide dough in half. Roll one half of dough on lightly floured work surface into 12×9-inch rectangle. Spread half of date mixture over dough. Spread evenly, leaving ¼-inch border on top short edge. Starting at short side, tightly roll up dough jelly-roll style. Wrap in plastic wrap; freeze for at least 1 hour. Repeat with remaining dough.

4. Preheat oven to 350°F. Grease cookie sheets. Unwrap dough. Using heavy thread or dental floss, cut dough into ¼-inch slices. Place slices 1 inch apart on prepared cookie sheets.

5. Bake 12 minutes or until lightly browned. Let cookies stand on cookie sheets 2 minutes. Remove cookies to wire rack; cool completely.

Makes 6 dozen cookies

Christmas Cookie Pops

1 package (20 ounces)
refrigerated sugar
cookie dough
All-purpose flour
(optional)
20 to 24 (4-inch) lollipop
sticks
Royal Icing (page 66)
6 ounces almond bark
(vanilla or chocolate), or
butterscotch chips
Vegetable shortening
Assorted small candies

1. Preheat oven to 350°F. Grease cookie sheets; set aside.

2. Remove dough from wrapper according to package directions.

3. Sprinkle dough with flour to minimize sticking, if necessary. Cut dough in half. Reserve 1 half; refrigerate remaining dough.

4. Roll reserved dough to $1/3$-inch thickness. Cut out cookies using $3\frac{1}{4}$- or $3\frac{1}{2}$-inch Christmas cookie cutters. Place lollipop sticks on cookies so that tips of sticks are imbedded in cookies. Carefully turn cookies with spatula so sticks are in back; place on prepared cookie sheets. Repeat with remaining dough.

5. Bake 7 to 11 minutes or until edges are lightly browned. Cool cookies on sheets 2 minutes. Remove cookies to wire racks; cool completely.

6. Prepare Royal Icing.

7. Melt almond bark in medium microwavable bowl according to package directions. Add 1 or more tablespoons shortening if coating is too thick. Hold cookies over bowl; spoon coating over cookies. Scrape excess coating from cookie edges. Decorate with small candies and Royal Icing immediately. Place cookies on wire racks set over waxed paper; let harden. Store in tin at room temperature.

Makes 20 to 24 cookies

Molasses Spice Cookies

    1 cup granulated sugar
    ¾ cup shortening
    ¼ cup molasses
    1 large egg, beaten
    2 cups all-purpose flour
    2 teaspoons baking soda
    1 teaspoon ground
        cinnamon
    1 teaspoon ground cloves
    1 teaspoon ground ginger
    ¼ teaspoon dry mustard
    ¼ teaspoon salt
    ½ cup granulated brown
        sugar

1. Preheat oven to 375°F. Grease cookie sheets; set aside.

2. Beat granulated sugar and shortening about 5 minutes in large bowl until light and fluffy. Add molasses and egg; beat until fluffy.

3. Combine flour, baking soda, cinnamon, cloves, ginger, mustard and salt in medium bowl. Add to shortening mixture; mix until just combined.

4. Place brown sugar in shallow dish. Roll tablespoonfuls of dough into 1-inch balls; roll in sugar to coat. Place 2 inches apart on prepared cookie sheets. Bake 15 minutes or until lightly browned. Let cookies stand on cookie sheets 2 minutes. Remove cookies to wire racks; cool completely.

Makes about 6 dozen cookies

HELPFUL HINTS

Looking for something different to take to all your holiday gatherings? Decorate a metal tin with rubber stamps for a crafty look and fill it with Molasses Spice Cookies and an assortment of uniquely flavored teas. Perfect for a twist on your traditional hostess gift.

Mincemeat Pastries

3½ cups all-purpose flour
¾ cup granulated sugar
½ teaspoon salt
½ cup (1 stick) butter, chilled
8 tablespoons vegetable shortening
1 cup buttermilk
1 cup mincemeat
¼ cup powdered sugar (optional)

1. Combine flour, granulated sugar and salt in large bowl; set aside.

2. Cut butter into 1-inch chunks. Add butter and shortening to flour mixture. Cut in with pastry blender or 2 knives until mixture resembles coarse crumbs. Drizzle buttermilk over top; toss just until mixture comes together into a ball.

3. Turn out dough onto lightly floured work surface; fold in half and flatten to about ½ inch thick. Knead about eight times. Divide dough in half; press each half into ½-inch-thick disk. Wrap in plastic wrap and refrigerate at least 30 minutes.

4. Preheat oven to 350°F. Lightly grease cookie sheets; set aside. Let dough rest at room temperature 10 minutes. Roll one disk of dough into 18×12-inch rectangle on lightly floured work surface. Cut into 24 (3-inch) squares. Place heaping ½ teaspoon mincemeat in center of each square. Fold one corner about ⅔ of the way over the filling; fold opposite corner ⅔ of the way over the filling.

5. Place 2 inches apart on prepared cookie sheets. Repeat with remaining dough.

6. Bake 20 minutes or until lightly browned. Remove cookies to wire rack; cool completely. Sprinkle tops of pastries lightly with powdered sugar.

Makes 4 dozen cookies

Chocolate Nut Bars

½ cup **uncooked quick oats**
½ cup **hazelnuts**
½ cup **walnuts**
¾ cup **powdered sugar**
 8 ounces (1¼ cups)
   **semisweet chocolate
   chips**
 1 tablespoon **vegetable
   shortening**
 2 tablespoons **butter**
½ teaspoon **salt**
⅓ cup **corn syrup**
½ teaspoon **vanilla**

1. Preheat oven to 350°F. Line an 8-inch square baking pan with foil, pressing foil into corners to cover completely and leaving 1-inch overhang on sides.

2. Spread oats on baking sheet. Bake 8 to 10 minutes or until light golden brown. Transfer oats to large bowl when cool. *Reduce oven temperature to 325°F.* Chop hazelnuts into uniform pieces. Spread on baking sheet. Bake 9 to 11 minutes or just until cut sides begin to brown lightly. Transfer to bowl with toasted oats when cool. Chop walnuts into uniform pieces; add to oat mixture. Stir in powdered sugar; set aside.

3. Heat chocolate chips with shortening in heavy small saucepan over very low heat, stirring constantly, until melted and smooth. Remove from heat. Spread evenly onto bottom of prepared pan with rubber spatula. Let stand in cool place about 15 to 20 minutes or until it begins to set, but is not firm.

4. Combine butter and salt in microwavable bowl. Microwave at HIGH 20 to 30 seconds or until butter is melted and foamy. Stir in corn syrup; let cool slightly and add vanilla. Stir corn syrup mixture into oat mixture just until moistened. Gently spoon over chocolate, spreading evenly into corners. Score lightly into 4 strips, then score each strip into 6 pieces. Cover tightly with plastic wrap and refrigerate until firm, at least 4 hours.

5. Remove from pan by lifting foil by edges. Place on cutting board; cut along score lines into 24 pieces. Remove from foil. Store in airtight container in refrigerator.   *Makes 24 bars*

Black and White Caramels

CARAMELS
2 cups sugar
2 cups light corn syrup
1 cup half-and-half
1 cup unsalted butter
½ teaspoon salt
1 cup whipping cream
1 teaspoon vanilla

COATING
12 ounces semisweet
    chocolate, chopped
14 to 16 ounces white
    chocolate, chopped and
    divided
6 teaspoons shortening

1. To prepare caramels, line 8-inch square pan with heavy-duty foil, pressing foil into corners to cover completely and leaving 1-inch overhang on sides. Lightly butter foil.

2. Combine sugar, corn syrup, half-and-half, butter and salt in heavy 4½-quart saucepan. Bring to a boil over medium-high heat, stirring occasionally. Wash down sugar crystals with pastry brush, if necessary. Continue boiling 25 minutes or until sugar mixture reaches firm-ball stage (244° to 246°F) on candy thermometer, stirring frequently. Remove from heat; very gradually stir in cream.

3. Return to medium heat. Cook 15 minutes or until mixture reaches 248°F on candy thermometer, stirring frequently. Remove from heat; stir in vanilla. Immediately pour into prepared pan. (Do not scrape saucepan.) Cool at room temperature 3 to 4 hours until firm.

4. Remove from pan by lifting caramels using foil handles. Place on cutting board; peel off foil. Cut into 1-inch strips with long thin bladed knife. Cut each strip into 1-inch squares with buttered knife or kitchen shears. Line two 13×9-inch baking pans with waxed paper; lightly butter paper. Place squares into prepared pans spacing each ¾ inch apart. Cover tightly with plastic wrap and let stand overnight at room temperature.

5. To prepare coating, temper semisweet chocolate according to directions on page 5. Lower caramels into tempered chocolate with dipping fork or spoon (do not pierce), tapping handle gently against side of pan to allow excess chocolate to drain back into pan. Remove excess chocolate by scraping bottom of caramel across rim of saucepan.

6. Place caramels on waxed paper. Let stand in cool place until chocolate is firm. (Do not refrigerate.)

7. Place 12 ounces of white chocolate and all of shortening in a clean double boiler; temper according to directions on page 5. Dip remaining caramels as directed in Step 5. As soon as white chocolate starts to thicken too much, return top pan to double boiler momentarily; stir in 1 additional ounce of white chocolate until mixture loosens without exceeding recommended temperature. Continue dipping, adding remaining white chocolate as needed periodically, until all caramels are coated.

8. Store coated caramels in airtight container at room temperature.

Makes 64 chocolate coated 1-inch caramels

Black and White Caramels

Butterscotch Patties

**1 cup firmly packed light
    brown sugar**
¼ cup butter
**2 tablespoons dark corn
    syrup**
1 tablespoon water
1 tablespoon cider vinegar
Pinch of salt

1. Line 2 baking sheets with foil.

2. Combine all ingredients in heavy 2-quart saucepan. Bring to a boil over medium-high heat, stirring constantly.

3. To wash down sugar crystals, dip pastry brush in hot water. Gently brush crystals down into sugar mixture or let them collect on brush bristles. Dip brush frequently into hot water to clean off bristles.

4. Continue boiling about 15 minutes or until sugar mixture reaches hard-crack stage (300° to 305°F) on candy thermometer, stirring frequently. (Watch carefully so that mixture does not burn.) Remove from heat; stir until mixture stops bubbling.

5. Quickly drop teaspoonfuls onto prepared baking sheets to form patties. Cool patties completely, about 15 minutes. Store in airtight container at room temperature between sheets of waxed paper.

Makes about 3 dozen 1½-inch patties (about ½ pound)

Butterscotch Pieces: *Prepare sugar mixture as directed. Pour onto foil instead of dropping into patties; cool completely and break into pieces. Store as directed.*

Molasses Chips: *Substitute light molasses for the dark corn syrup. Proceed as directed.*

Butterscotch Pieces

Double-Chocolate Coffee Balls

1 can (8 ounces) almond paste
3 tablespoons bourbon
1 egg white
3 cups powdered sugar, divided
54 to 56 purchased chocolate-coated coffee beans
16 ounces premium semisweet or bittersweet chocolate, chopped
⅔ cup heavy cream

1. Beat almond paste, bourbon and egg white in medium bowl with electric mixer at medium speed until blended. Add 2 cups powdered sugar; beat at low speed until well mixed. Place on surface dusted with powdered sugar. Knead in remaining 1 cup powdered sugar until smooth. Shape into two 1¼-inch diameter logs. Cut one ¼-inch slice from log. Flatten slightly into a circle. Sprinkle work surface with powdered sugar as needed to prevent sticking. Keep logs covered with plastic wrap until ready to cut.

2. Place coffee bean in center of slice; fold sides up around coffee bean. With fingertips, smooth into ball. Set on tray lined with waxed paper. Cover lightly with plastic wrap. Repeat steps with remaining logs until all the balls are made. Place in freezer.

3. Fill bottom pan of double boiler with water to 1 inch below level of top pan. Bring water just to a boil; reduce heat to low. Place chocolate in top of double boiler. Stir until chocolate is melted. While chocolate is melting, bring heavy cream to a boil over medium-high heat in small saucepan. Remove from heat. Add hot cream all at once to melted chocolate; whisk quickly until mixture is smooth and glossy (the initial graininess will disperse). Check temperature of chocolate with candy thermometer and maintain between 125° to 130°F while dipping.

4. Remove tray from freezer. Dip balls into melted chocolate with dipping fork or spoon, tapping handle a few times against side of pan to allow excess chocolate to drain back into pan. Remove excess chocolate by scraping bottom of ball across rim of saucepan. Place balls back on waxed paper. Let stand in cool place 20 minutes; refrigerate 1 hour. Gently remove balls from waxed paper and place in foil cups. Store in airtight container in freezer or refrigerator.

Makes about 4½ dozen balls

Double-Chocolate Coffee Balls

Elegant Holiday Holly Mints

1 package (3 ounces) cream
  cheese, softened
3 tablespoons butter or
  margarine, softened
3 teaspoons liquid green
  food coloring
½ teaspoon vanilla
¼ teaspoon peppermint
  extract
1 pound powdered sugar
  (3½ to 4 cups)
½ cup granulated sugar
1 jar (2 ounces) cinnamon
  candies

1. Line large cookie sheet with waxed paper; set aside.

2. Beat cream cheese, butter, food coloring, vanilla and peppermint extract in large bowl with electric mixer at medium speed until smooth. Gradually beat in powdered sugar on low speed until well combined, scraping side of bowl several times. (If necessary stir in remaining powdered sugar with wooden spoon.) Turn out cream cheese mixture onto sheet of waxed paper lightly sprinkled with powdered sugar. Knead dough until smooth and pliable. Place granulated sugar in shallow bowl; set aside.

3. Shape dough into 8½ × 2¼-inch block. Cut ½-inch slice with long thin bladed knife. Place slice on another sheet of waxed paper; flatten gently with fingertips to 3½-inch oval about ¼ inch thick.

4. Transfer slice to bowl with granulated sugar; flip to coat both sides. Return slice to waxed paper; cut two 1½-inch leaves out of slice or use miniature 1½-inch cookie cutter. (If dough becomes too soft to work with, wrap in plastic wrap and refrigerate for 15 minutes.) Press cinnamon candies firmly into leaf to resemble berries. Repeat steps with remaining dough and scraps. Place on prepared cookie sheets; refrigerate until firm. Store in airtight container in refrigerator.

*Makes about 60 (1½-inch)
holly leaf mints*

Double-Chocolate Strawberry Triangles

⅓ **portion prepared Strawberry Sour Cream Fondant (page 87)**
1¼ **cups semisweet chocolate chips**
1¼ **cups milk chocolate chips**

1. Line 8-inch square pan with foil leaving 1-inch overhang on sides.

2. Roll out prepared fondant on sheet of waxed paper to an 8-inch square; use fingertips to form right angles at corners. Cover with plastic wrap; set aside.

3. Heat semisweet chocolate chips in small heavy saucepan over very low heat until melted and smooth. Pour onto bottom of prepared pan; spread evenly, ½ inch from pan edges.

4. Remove plastic; fold fondant in half, fondant side out. Place fondant half directly on top of one half of melted chocolate. Flip remaining side over; press down gently and evenly all over, including corners so that all chocolate and fondant edges meet. Peel away waxed paper. Cover with plastic wrap and refrigerate 20 to 30 minutes or just until firm.

5. Heat milk chocolate chips in small heavy saucepan over very low heat until melted and smooth. Pour over fondant layer, smoothing to all edges and corners evenly. Let stand at room temperature 45 minutes or until set. After the first 10 minutes, score lightly into 16 (2-inch) squares, then score each square diagonally into 2 triangles.

6. Remove chocolate triangles and foil from pan by foil handles. Place on cutting board; peel foil down from sides. Gently transfer triangles to board. To finish cutting, score each triangle on the diagonal in half again, then gently cut through to make 2 smaller triangles. Store in airtight container in refrigerator.

Makes 64 Double Chocolate-Strawberry Triangles

STRAWBERRY SOUR CREAM FONDANT

- ⅓ cup butter, softened
- ¼ cup sour cream
- 1½ tablespoons creme de strawberry liqueur
- ⅛ teaspoon salt
- 1½ (1-pound) packages (about 6 cups) strawberry-flavored powdered sugar or regular powdered sugar, sifted and divided

1. Combine butter, sour cream, strawberry liqueur and salt in large bowl; beat with electric mixer at medium speed until smooth. Add ½ of powdered sugar; beat well.

2. Stir in enough remaining powdered sugar with wooden spoon to make mixture stiff. Turn out powdered sugar mixture onto countertop or cutting board. Knead dough until smooth and pliable. Shape into rectangular block. Cut off one third of dough; set aside. Wrap remaining two thirds dough in plastic wrap and reserve in refrigerator for another use.

Double-Chocolate Strawberry Triangles

Triple Layer Fudge

Chocolate Fudge (recipe follows)
Peanut Butter Fudge (recipe follows)
White Fudge (recipe follows)

1. Grease 13×9-inch baking pan; set aside. Prepare Chocolate Fudge. Immediately spread into prepared pan with lightly greased rubber spatula.

2. Immediately prepare Peanut Butter Fudge; spread evenly over Chocolate Fudge with lightly greased rubber spatula.

3. Immediately prepare White Fudge; spread evenly over Peanut Butter Fudge with lightly greased spatula.

4. If desired, to marble fudge, swirl knife through all layers, lifting and turning fudges with each swirl.

5. Cover fudge with plastic wrap. Refrigerate 2 hours or until firm. Cut into 1-inch squares. Store tightly covered in refrigerator up to 3 weeks.

Makes about 10 dozen pieces

CHOCOLATE FUDGE

1½ cups sugar
1 can (5 ounces) evaporated milk
2 tablespoons butter
¼ teaspoon salt
1½ cups miniature marshmallows
1 cup (6 ounces) semisweet chocolate chips
1½ teaspoons vanilla

1. Combine sugar, milk, butter and salt in medium saucepan. Bring to a boil over medium heat, stirring constantly. Boil 5 minutes, stirring constantly.

2. Remove saucepan from heat. Stir in marshmallows until melted and mixture is blended.

3. Add chocolate chips and vanilla. Stir until mixture is smooth. Stir mixture 6 minutes or until slightly thickened.

Peanut Butter Fudge: *Reduce granulated sugar to ¾ cup; add ¾ cup packed light brown sugar. Omit butter and chocolate. Prepare as directed for Chocolate Fudge in Steps 1 and 2. Stir ½ cup creamy peanut butter into mixture as directed in Step 3.*

White Fudge: *Substitute white chocolate chips for semisweet chocolate chips. Prepare as directed for Chocolate Fudge.*

Caramel-Nut Chocolate Cups

36 Chocolate Cups (recipe follows) or purchased chocolate liqueur cups
¾ cup plus 36 pecan halves, divided
¾ cup caramel-flavored topping
1⅛ cups semisweet chocolate chips
1½ teaspoons vegetable shortening

1. Prepare Chocolate Cups; set aside.

2. Preheat oven to 375°F. Spread pecans on baking sheet. Bake 8 to 10 minutes or until golden brown, stirring frequently. Remove from baking sheet; cool. Chop ¾ cup pecan halves into uniform pieces. Reserve 36 pecan halves.

3. Spoon scant 1 teaspoon caramel topping into each Chocolate Cup. Top each with 1 teaspoon chopped pecans, pressing gently; set aside.

4. Fill bottom pan of double boiler with water to 1 inch below level of top pan. Bring water just to a boil; reduce heat to low. Place chocolate and shortening in top of double boiler. Stir until chocolate is melted. Remove from heat.

5. Spoon scant 1 teaspoon melted chocolate around perimeter of each cup; smooth toward center until cup is fully covered. Immediately place one toasted pecan half in center. Let stand in cool place until firm. Store at room temperature in airtight container.

Makes 36 Caramel-Nut Chocolate Cups

CHOCOLATE CUPS

1 package (12 ounces) semisweet chocolate chips
1 tablespoon vegetable shortening

1. Melt chocolate chips and shortening in small saucepan over very low heat, stirring constantly. Remove from heat.

2. Spoon about ½ tablespoon melted chocolate into each of 36 small foil candy cups. Brush chocolate up side of each cup with clean paintbrush, coating foil completely. Carefully wipe off any chocolate that may have run over top using tip of finger. Place cups on baking sheet; let stand in cool place until firm. (Do not refrigerate.)

3. To remove foil cups, cut slits in bottom of foil cups and peel foil up from bottom.

Black Russian Truffles

8 ounces premium bittersweet chocolate, broken into 2-inch pieces
¼ cup whipping cream
2 tablespoons butter
3½ tablespoons coffee-flavored liqueur
1½ tablespoons vodka
1 cup chopped toasted walnuts

1. Place chocolate in food processor; process until chocolate is chopped.

2. Combine cream and butter in 1-cup glass measuring cup. Microwave at HIGH 1½ minutes or until butter is melted and cream begins to boil.

3. With food processor running, pour hot cream mixture through food tube; process until chocolate melts.

4. Add liqueur and vodka; process until blended. Pour chocolate mixture into medium bowl; cover with plastic wrap and refrigerate overnight.

5. Shape chocolate mixture into 1-inch balls. Roll in walnuts.

6. Store in airtight container in refrigerator. Let stand at room temperature 2 to 3 hours before serving.

Makes about 2½ dozen truffles

Brandy Truffles: *Add 3½ tablespoons brandy to chocolate mixture in Step 4 in place of coffee-flavored liqueur and vodka. Roll truffles in 1 cup powdered sugar in place of walnuts.*

Hazelnut Truffles: *Add 3½ tablespoons hazelnut-flavored liqueur and 1½ tablespoons gold tequila to chocolate mixture in Step 4 in place of coffee-flavored liqueur and vodka. Roll truffles in 1 cup chopped toasted hazelnuts in place of walnuts.*

Black Russian Truffles, Brandy Truffles and Hazelnut Truffles

 # Index

VOLUME MEASUREMENTS (dry)

1/8 teaspoon = 0.5 mL

1/4 teaspoon = 1 mL

1/2 teaspoon = 2 mL

3/4 teaspoon = 4 mL

1 teaspoon = 5 mL

1 tablespoon = 15 mL

2 tablespoons = 30 mL

1/4 cup = 60 mL

1/3 cup = 75 mL

1/2 cup = 125 mL

2/3 cup = 150 mL

3/4 cup = 175 mL

1 cup = 250 mL

2 cups = 1 pint = 500 mL

3 cups = 750 mL

4 cups = 1 quart = 1 L

VOLUME MEASUREMENTS (fluid)

1 fluid ounce (2 tablespoons) = 30 mL

4 fluid ounces (1/2 cup) = 125 mL

8 fluid ounces (1 cup) = 250 mL

12 fluid ounces (1 1/2 cups) = 375 mL

16 fluid ounces (2 cups) = 500 mL

WEIGHTS (mass)

1/2 ounce = 15 g

1 ounce = 30 g

3 ounces = 90 g

4 ounces = 120 g

8 ounces = 225 g

10 ounces = 285 g

12 ounces = 360 g

16 ounces = 1 pound = 450 g

DIMENSIONS

1/16 inch = 2 mm

1/8 inch = 3 mm

1/4 inch = 6 mm

1/2 inch = 1.5 cm

3/4 inch = 2 cm

1 inch = 2.5 cm

OVEN TEMPERATURES

250°F = 120°C

275°F = 140°C

300°F = 150°C

325°F = 160°C

350°F = 180°C

375°F = 190°C

400°F = 200°C

425°F = 220°C

450°F = 230°C

BAKING PAN SIZES

Utensil	Size in Inches/ Quarts	Metric Volume	Size in Centimeters
Baking or Cake Pan (square or rectangular)	8×8×2	2 L	20×20×5
	9×9×2	2.5 L	23×23×5
	12×8×2	3 L	30×20×5
	13×9×2	3.5 L	33×23×5
Loaf Pan	8×4×3	1.5 L	20×10×7
	9×5×3	2 L	23×13×7
Round Layer Cake Pan	8×1 1/2	1.2 L	20×4
	9×1 1/2	1.5 L	23×4
Pie Plate	8×1 1/4	750 mL	20×3
	9×1 1/4	1 L	23×3
Baking Dish or Casserole	1 quart	1 L	—
	1 1/2 quart	1.5 L	—
	2 quart	2 L	—